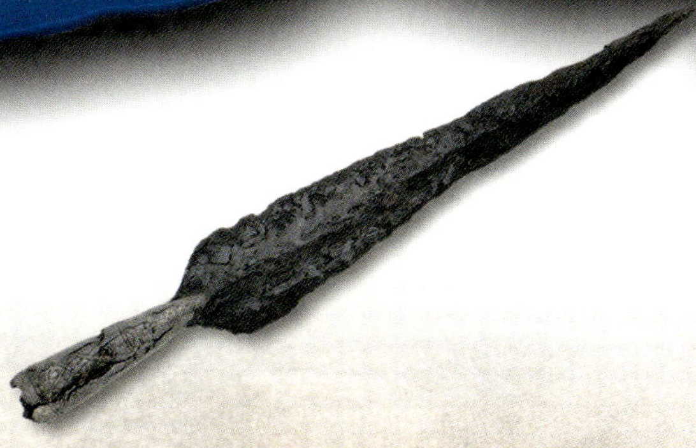

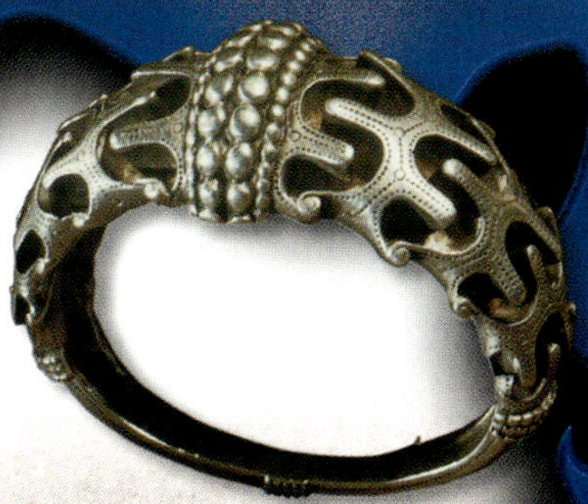

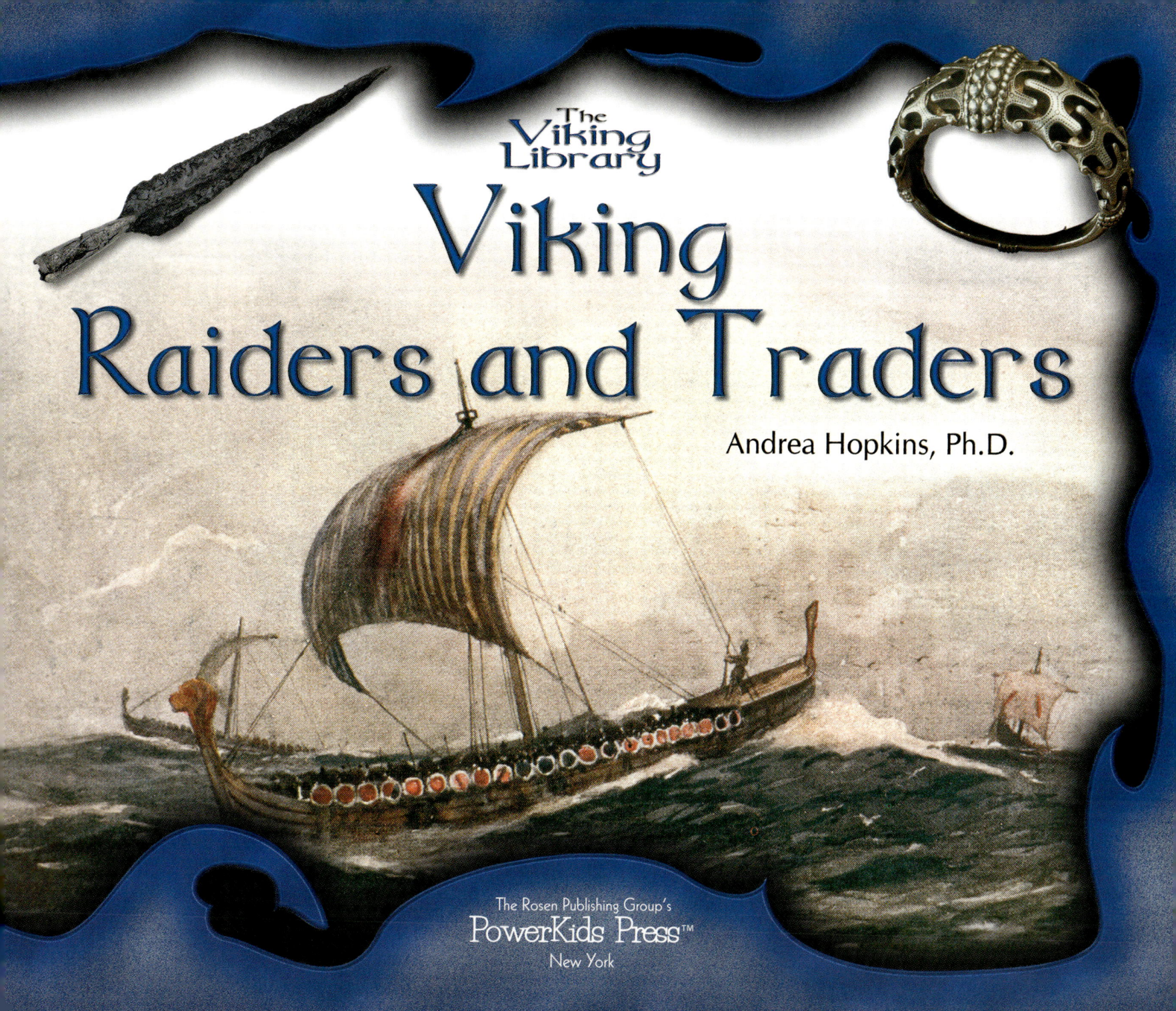

The Viking Library

Viking Raiders and Traders

Andrea Hopkins, Ph.D.

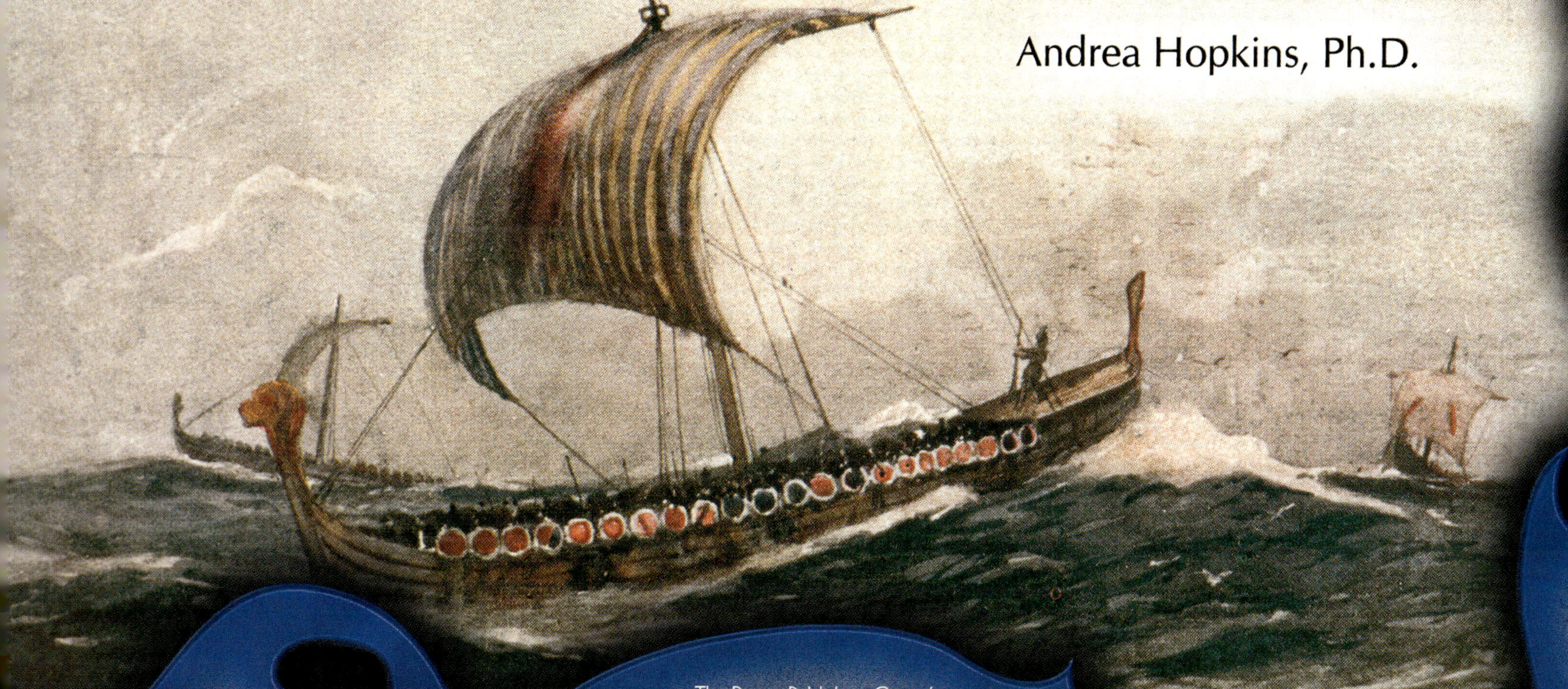

The Rosen Publishing Group's
PowerKids Press™
New York

To my brother Jonathan

Published in 2002 by The Rosen Publishing Group, Inc.
29 East 21st Street, New York, NY 10010

Copyright © 2002 by The Rosen Publishing Group, Inc.
All rights reserved. No part of this book may be reproduced in any form without permission from the publisher, except by a reviewer.

First Edition

Book Design: Michael Caroleo
Project Editor: Frances E. Ruffin

Photo Credits: Title page and p. 4 (longship sailing) © Mary Evans Picture Library; title page and p. 7 (spear) © Hulkkunanmaki, Lieto, Finland, National Board of Antiquities; title page (arm ring), contents page, pp. 15 (all), 16 (scale), 19 (Gokstad ship), 20 (pottery bowl) © Werner Forman Archive; p. 4 (map) © Map Art; p. 7 (Lindisfarne) © Macduff Everton/CORBIS; p. 8 (attack scene) © North Wind Pictures; p. 8 (Charles the Bald) © Archivo Iconografico, S.A./CORBIS; p. 11 (Birka) © Ted Spiegel/CORBIS; p. 11 (Birka hoard) © The Art Archive/Historiska Muséet Stockholm/Dagil Orti; p. 12 (Prince Rurik) © Bettmann/CORBIS; p. 12 (map) prepared by Marcia Bakry, NMNH; p. 16 (Kyrksundet Harbor) © National Board of Antiquities, Hannu Vallas; p. 19 (sword) © Matti Huuhka, Museokuva, National Board of Antiquities; p. 19 (street scene reconstruction) © York Archaeological Trust; p. 20 (beaded necklace) © Christian Ahlin, Museum of National Antiquities, Stockholm; p. 20 (hoard) courtesy of University Museum of Cultural Heritage, Oslo.

Images on cover(spear), title page (spear) and pp. 7 (spear), 12 (map), 16 (Kyrksundet Harbor), cover(sword), 19 (sword), 20 (beaded necklace and hoard) courtesy of the Arctic Studies Center, Smithsonian National Museum of Natural History.

Hopkins, Andrea.
Viking raiders and traders / Andrea Hopkins.—1st ed.
    p. cm. — (The Viking library)
Includes bibliographical references and index.
ISBN 0-8239-5813-2 (library binding)
1. Vikings—Juvenile literature. 2. Norsemen—Juvenile literature. I. Title. II. Series.
DL65 .H7 2002b
948'.22—dc21

2001001201

Manufactured in the United States of America

Contents

1	Raiding and Trading	5
2	Raiders: The Beginning	6
3	Big Raids in the West	9
4	Raiding Lands in the East	10
5	Attacking Constantinople	13
6	Viking Silver	14
7	Viking Merchants	17
8	Viking Goods for Sale	18
9	Imported Goods	21
10	Scandinavian Trading Centers	22
	Glossary	23
	Index	24
	Web Sites	24

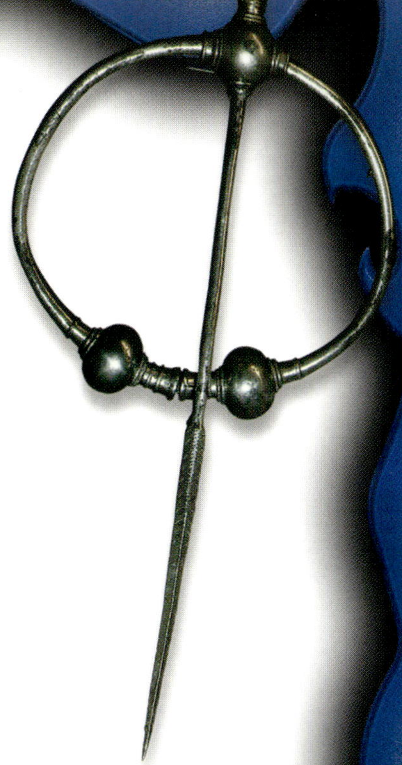

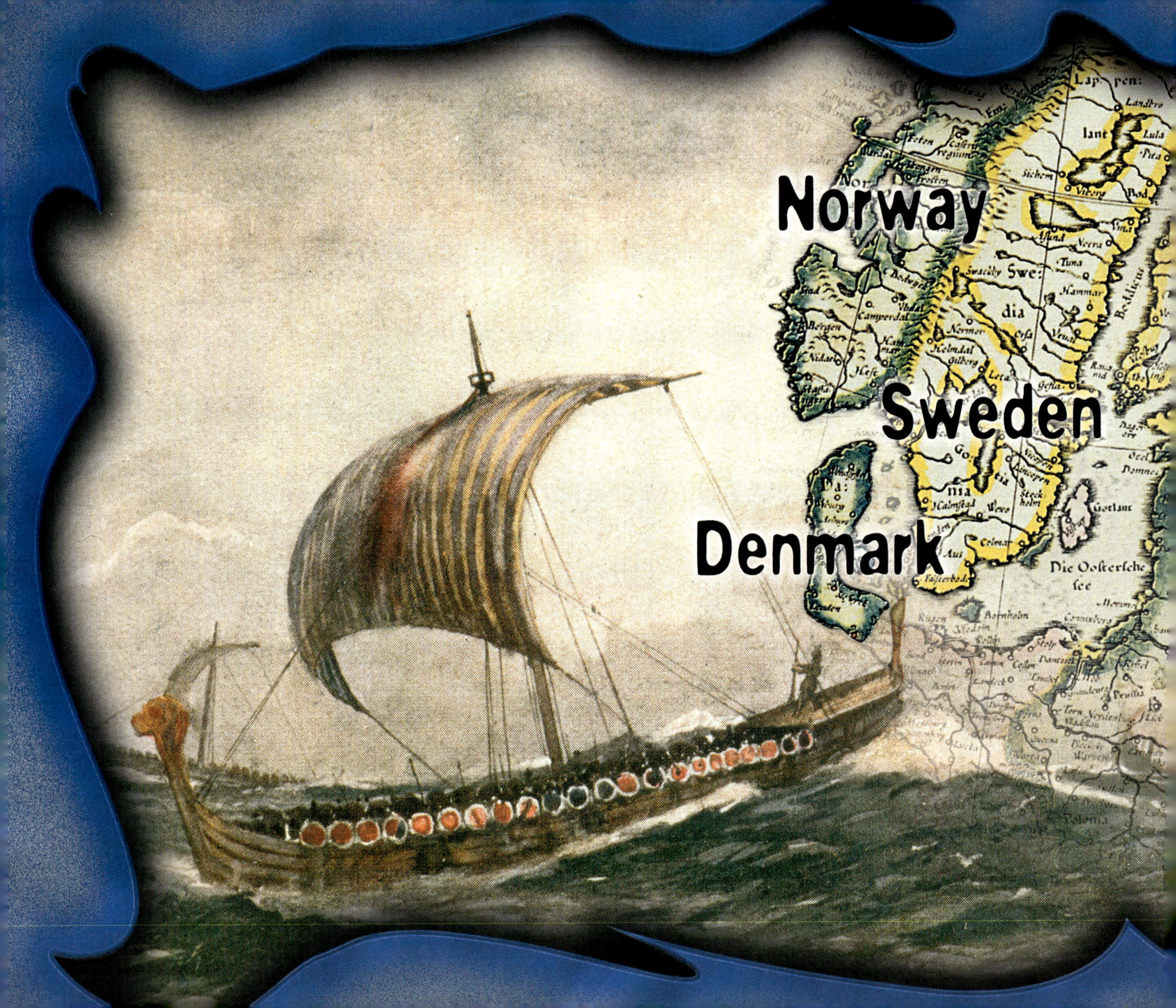
Norway
Sweden
Denmark

Raiding and Trading

Trading was an **essential** part of life for the Norse people. The Norse lived in Norway, Sweden, and Denmark. These are countries that we now call **Scandinavia**. In the eighth century, some Norse became Vikings. Vikings were what we might call pirates. They entered countries from the sea and moved up rivers. On the way, Vikings might have stolen cattle or other food that didn't belong to them. Soon they began to raid places to steal more valuable things.

During the Viking Age, from about A.D. 793 to A.D. 1066, Viking traders traveled to countries far from their own. There was almost no part of Europe that they couldn't reach.

Viking raiding parties traveled on light, easy-to-control longships, like the one in this painting. Also shown is a map of Scandinavia.

Raiders: The Beginning

The Vikings didn't begin suddenly to carry out raids in faraway countries. During the 600s and 700s, people in Norway, Sweden, and Denmark organized themselves into warlike, **tribal** groups. They stole cattle and attacked one another. They competed for the few **resources** in their cold, northern countries. The Vikings found out that there were **monasteries** in countries that lay to the west and south. These monasteries were full of treasure. The first recorded Viking raid on a monastery took place in June A.D. 793. The Vikings looted and burned Lindisfarne, a monastery on the coast of England. The Vikings carried off young, strong **monks** whom they could sell as **slaves**. The Vikings were fast and very dangerous.

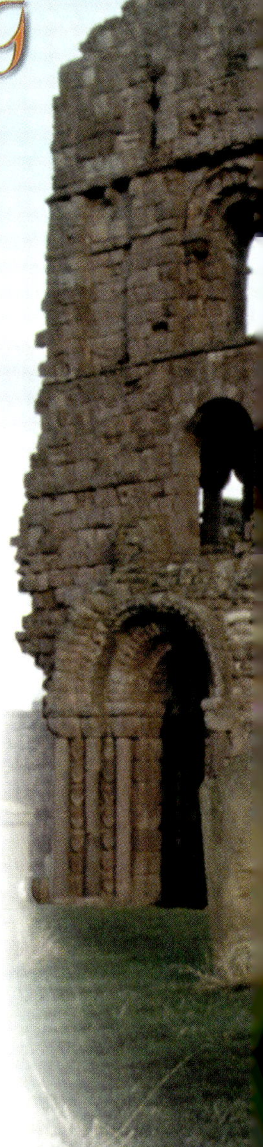

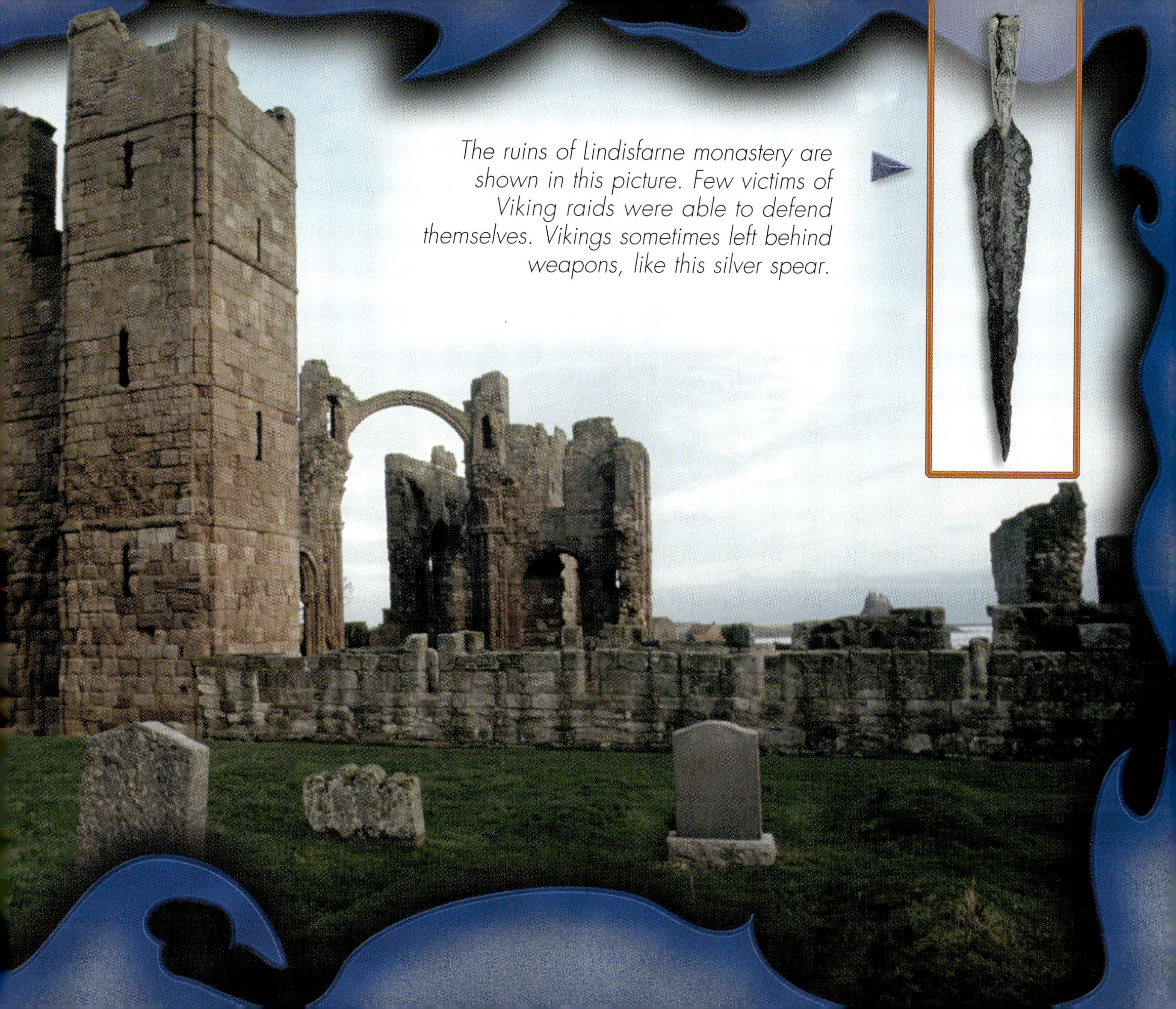

The ruins of Lindisfarne monastery are shown in this picture. Few victims of Viking raids were able to defend themselves. Vikings sometimes left behind weapons, like this silver spear.

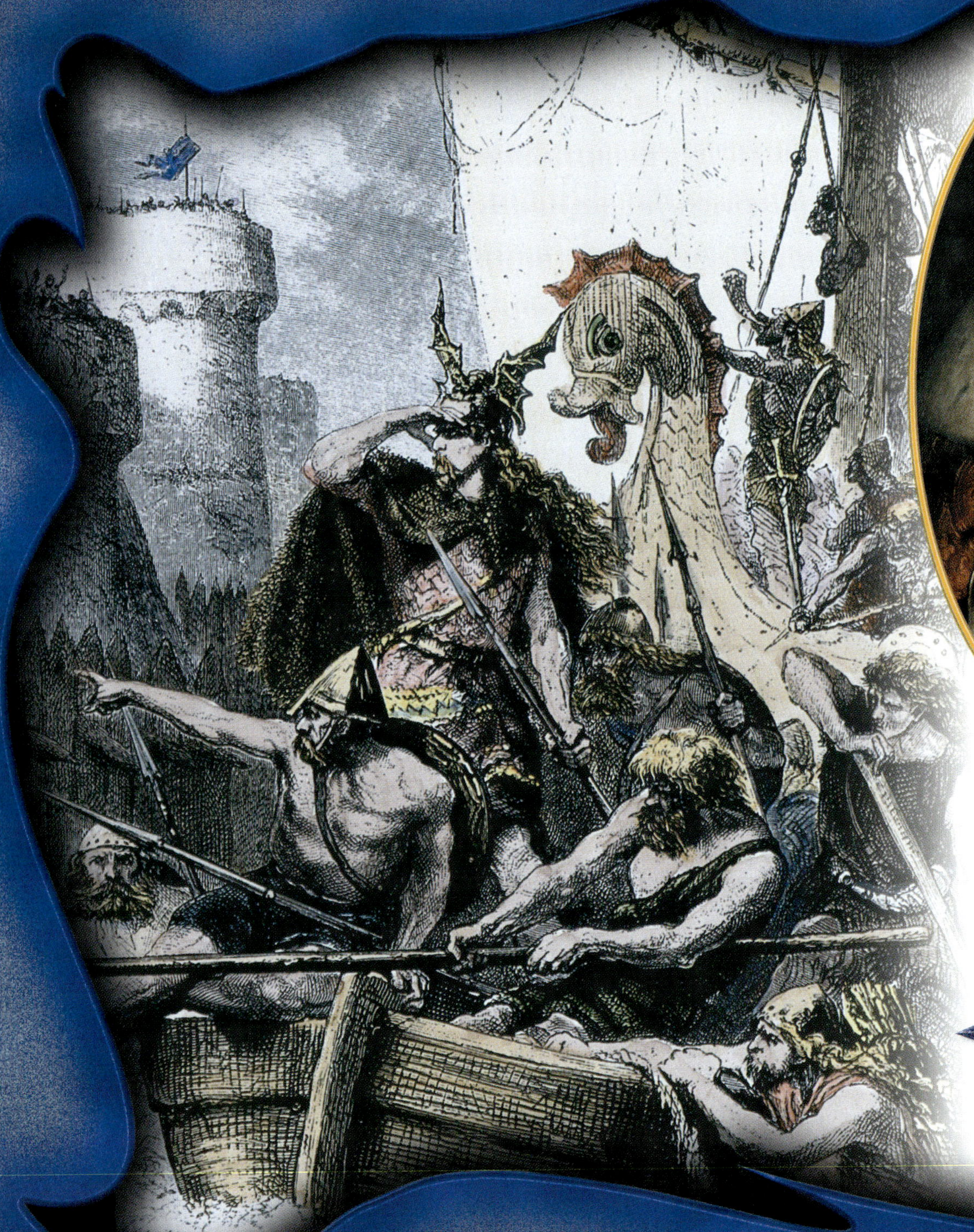

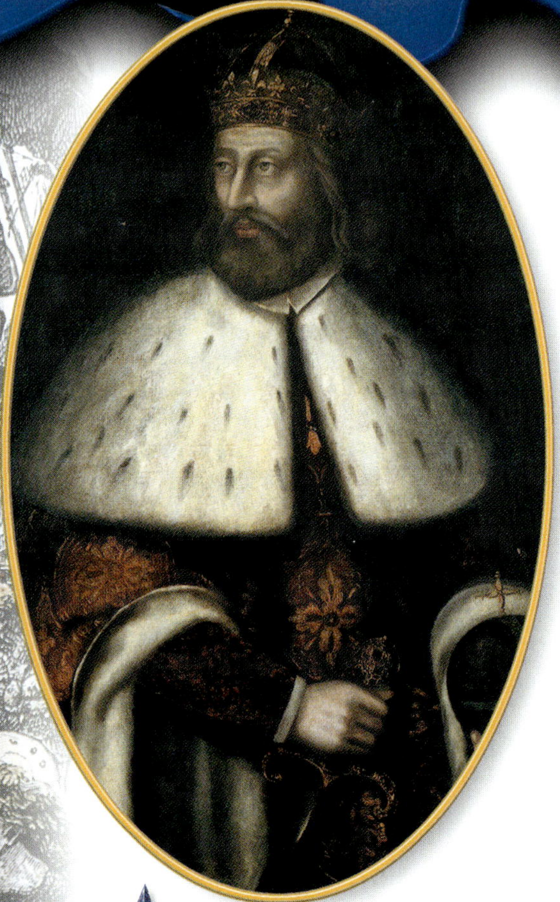

The painting by Filippo Aristo shows the French king, Charles the Bald, who tried to pay off the Vikings with danegeld.

The hand-colored woodcut shows the Viking leader known as Rollo the Ranger planning his attack on Paris.

Big Raids in the West

The Vikings soon turned their attention to rich, trading towns. These places were full of **foreign** goods and money. These towns were harder to attack because they were **fortified** and well defended. Soon bands of Vikings joined one another to form big **fleets** of ships. The ships contained great armies of men who carried out raids that were like major **invasions**. Charles the Bald, who ruled France from A.D. 840 to A.D. 877, bought his country some peace by paying the Vikings to go away. This arrangement was called danegeld. The French were forced to pay danegeld, or peace money, 13 times.

> England paid danegeld 26 times, but the Danish Vikings' king, Sven Forkbeard, led his army to conquer all of England in A.D. 1014. His son, Canute the Great, king of Denmark, became king of England.

Raiding Lands in the East

While the Danes and Norwegians raided western Europe, the Swedes sailed east. For many years, they had traded with their neighbors on the shores of the Baltic Sea. This sea surrounds Scandinavia. They traded with Finland and the Wends, people who lived in what is now eastern Germany. By the middle of the 800s, the Vikings sailed their longships down rivers that led them to the Ukraine and Russia. They went to trade and to raid. The route they chose was dangerous and difficult. Between rivers, the Vikings had to drag their ships over land on rollers. This made the Vikings open to attack from the people who lived there. To protect themselves, the Vikings set up well-fortified, well-defended trading stations that grew into powerful towns.

The remains of Birka, Sweden, an important Viking trading center, are shown here. The Viking silver coins and jewelry dating from A.D. 830 to A.D. 850 were uncovered at Birka.

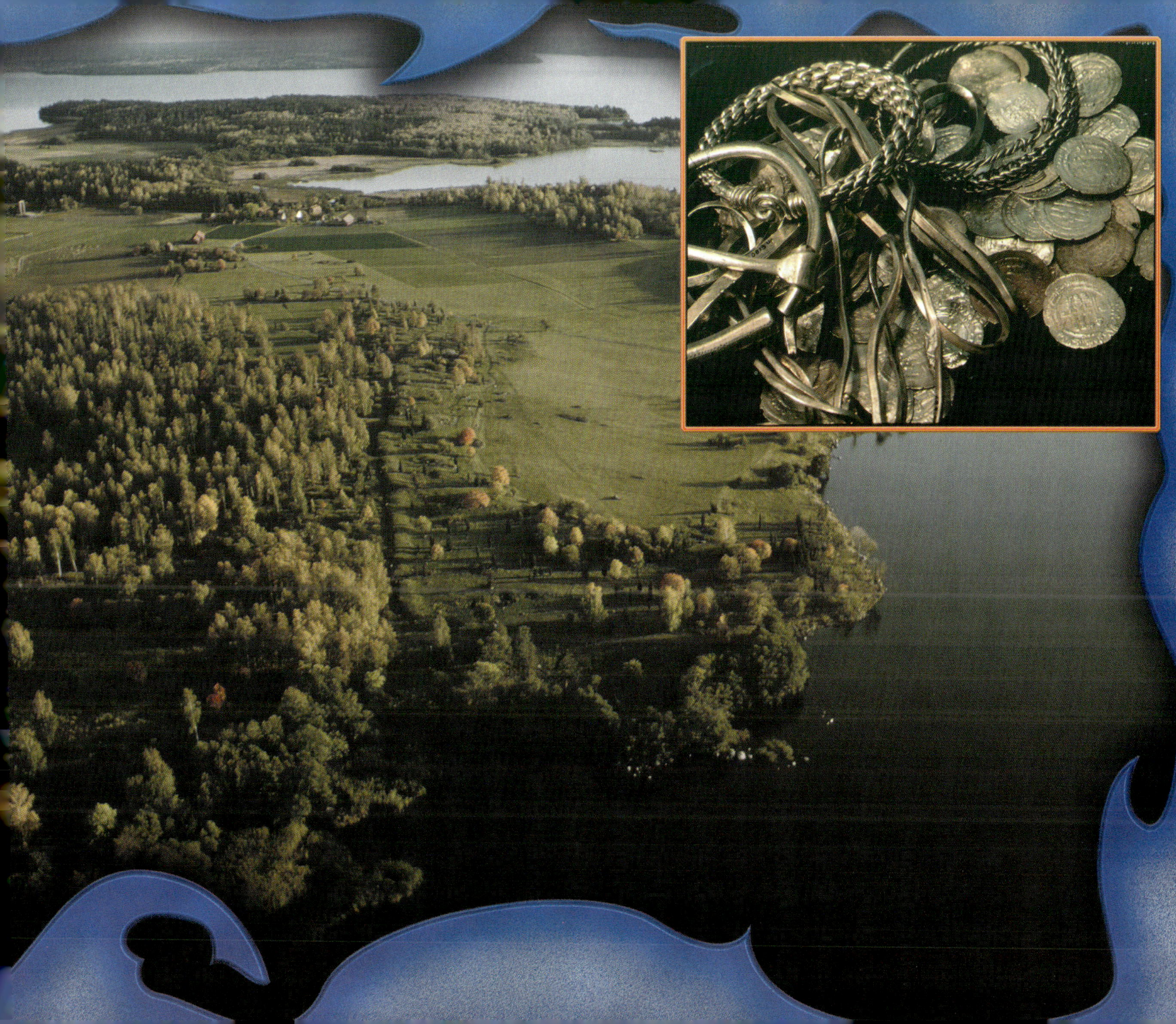

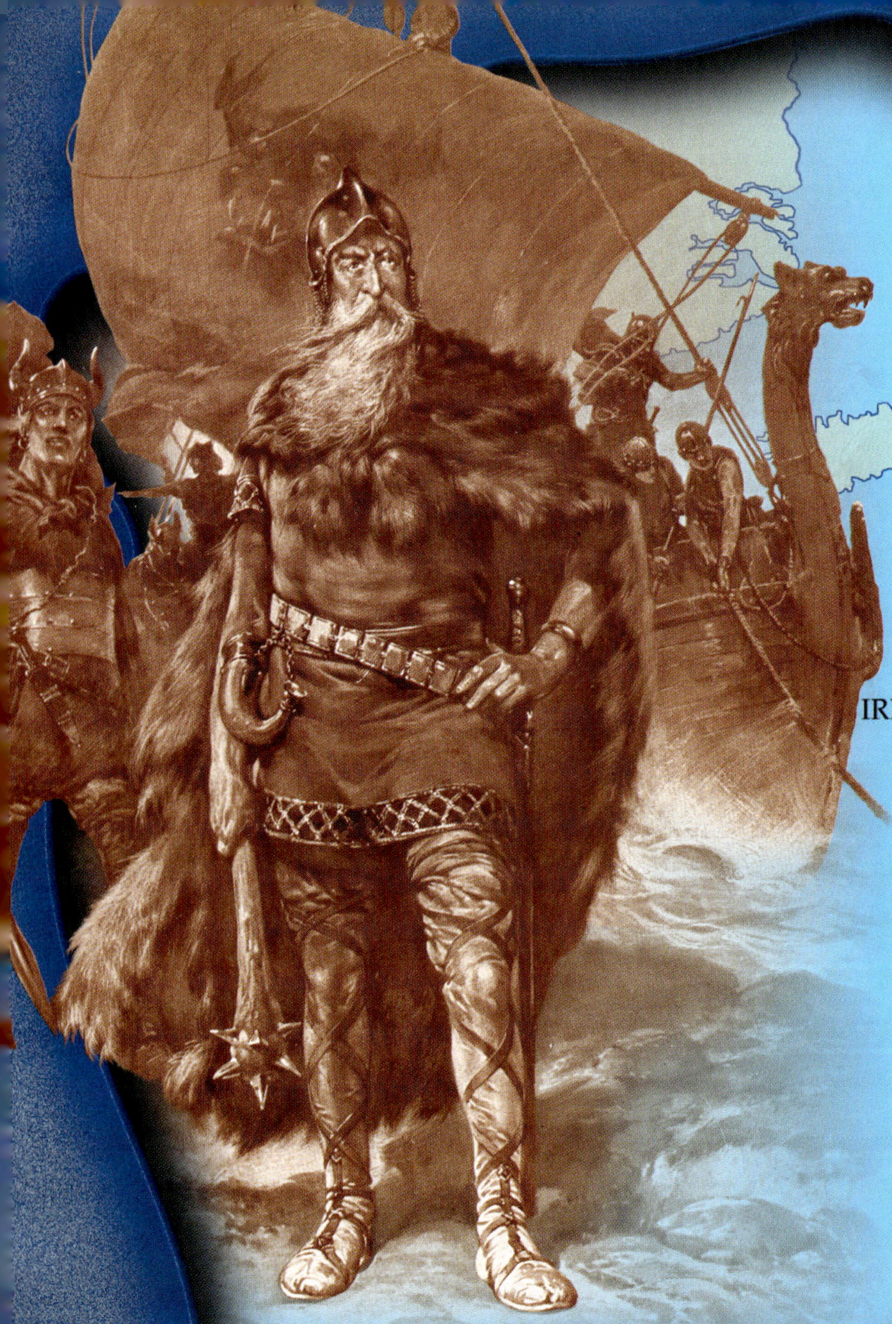

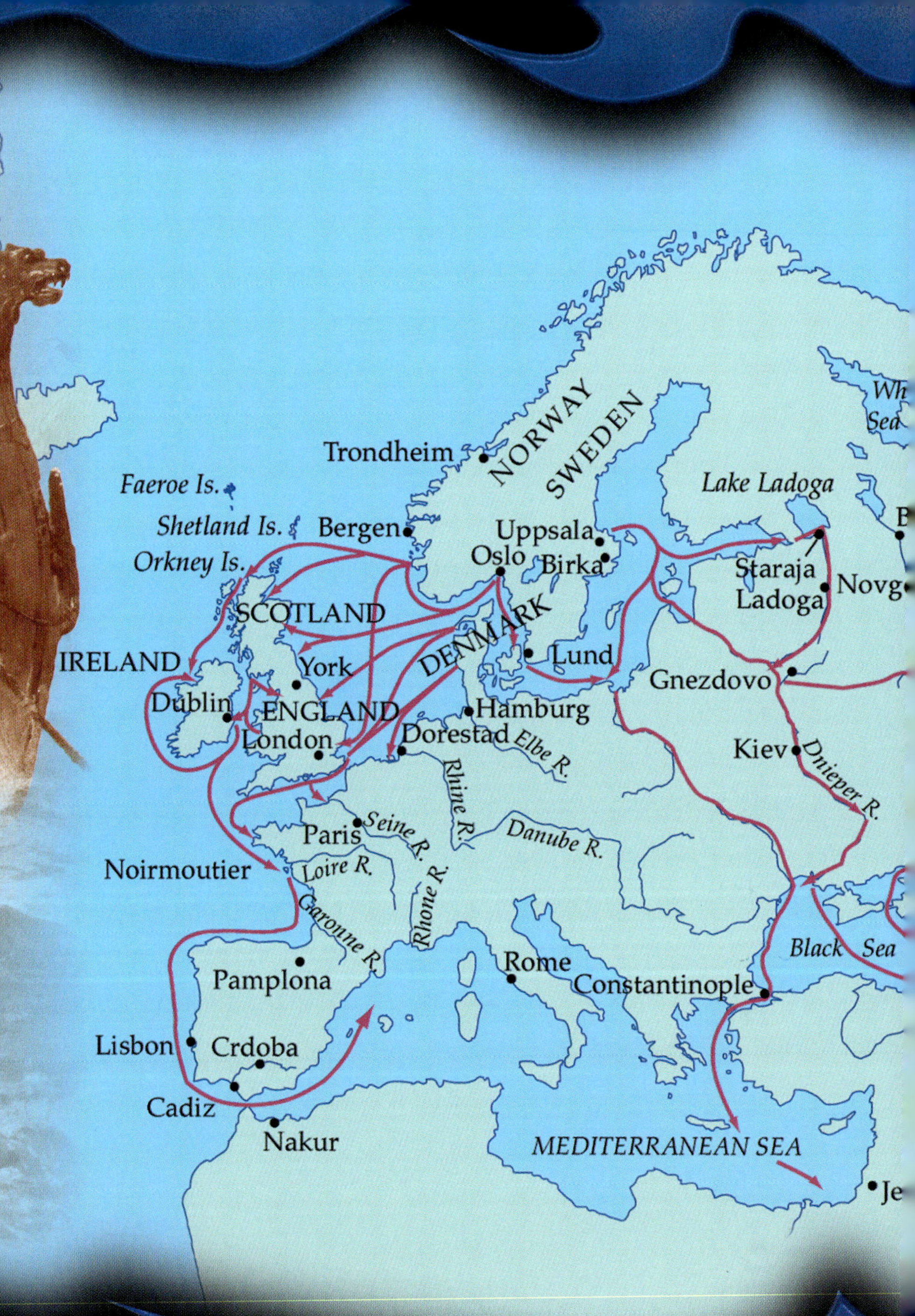

NORWAY
SWEDEN
Trondheim
Faeroe Is.
Shetland Is.
Bergen
Orkney Is.
Uppsala
Oslo
Birka
Lake Ladoga
Staraja
Ladoga
SCOTLAND
DENMARK
IRELAND
York
Lund
Gnezdovo
Dublin
ENGLAND
Hamburg
London
Dorestad
Elbe R.
Kiev
Dnieper R.
Rhine R.
Paris
Seine R.
Danube R.
Noirmoutier
Loire R.
Garonne R.
Rhone R.
Black Sea
Pamplona
Rome
Constantinople
Lisbon
Crdoba
Cadiz
Nakur
MEDITERRANEAN SEA

Attacking Constantinople

In A.D. 879, a Swedish Viking named Oleg the Wise became ruler of Novgorod, a trading town west of what is now Russia, and of Kiev in the Ukraine. The Swedes who settled in these lands were called the Rus. From Rus came the name Russia. In A.D. 907, Prince Oleg led a huge force of several hundred ships to conquer the rich and powerful city of Constantinople in the country of Turkey. At first the Vikings were barred from entering the city by a giant chain strung across the river. Oleg and his men put their ships on rollers and dragged them around the chain. Then the people of Constantinople made a trading treaty with the Vikings. They made a large cash payment to prevent their city from being looted for its riches.

 The image at the top left shows Rurik, a Swedish Viking leader who founded Russia. The map shows the route of Viking raids leading to the attack on Constantinople.

Viking Silver

Silver was the favorite form of **currency** for the Norse. They used it to buy goods or to save in **hoards**. Silver also was given as gifts and was collected to gain wealth. The Norse chopped their silver into small pieces, to be used in any shape or form. This was called hacksilver. At the beginning of the Viking age, the Norse didn't have coins like other people. There were no silver mines in Scandinavia, either. The Vikings left their homelands in search of silver and other treasure. With the silver that was brought back, the Norse people loved to make arm rings, brooches, and necklaces. Norse **craftsmen** made beautiful jewelry with designs of animals and plants.

> Some Norse collected treasure and buried it in the ground. No one is sure why. Archaeologists have dug up many such hoards. Some believe that the treasures were buried so they would not be stolen. Others believe that they might have been buried as religious offerings.

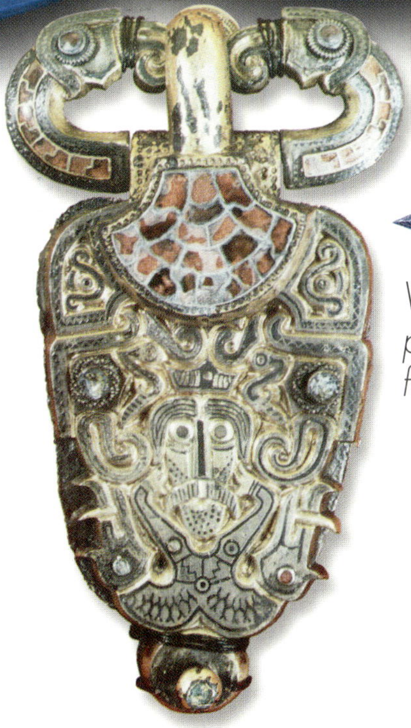

This seventeenth-century silver Viking brooch has precious stones. It was found in Norway.

This beautiful arm ring with dragon heads was created in Sweden during the eleventh century.

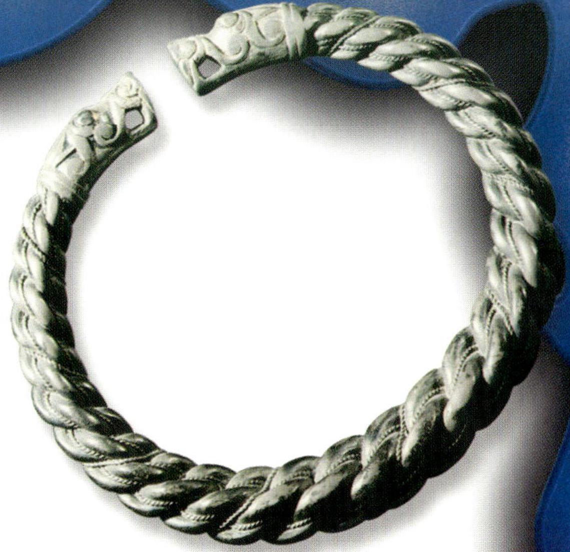

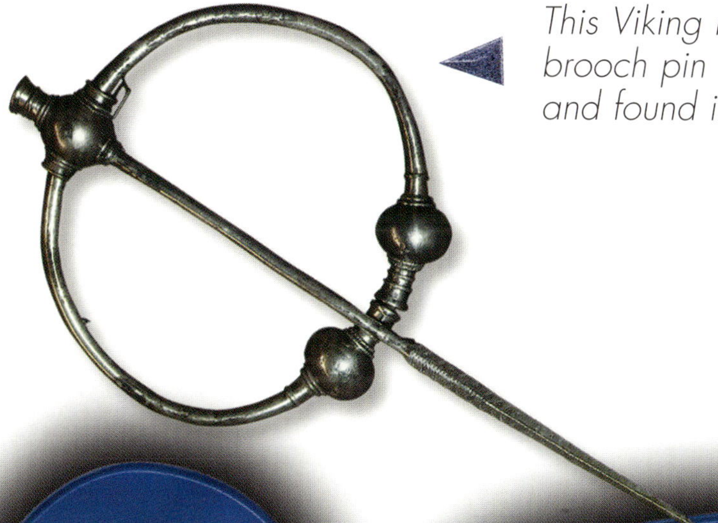

This Viking ring-and-brooch pin was made and found in Norway.

This beautifully designed arm ring was created in Denmark during the tenth century.

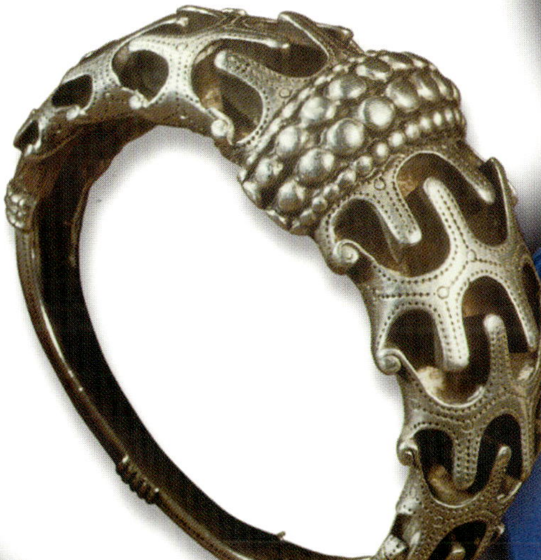

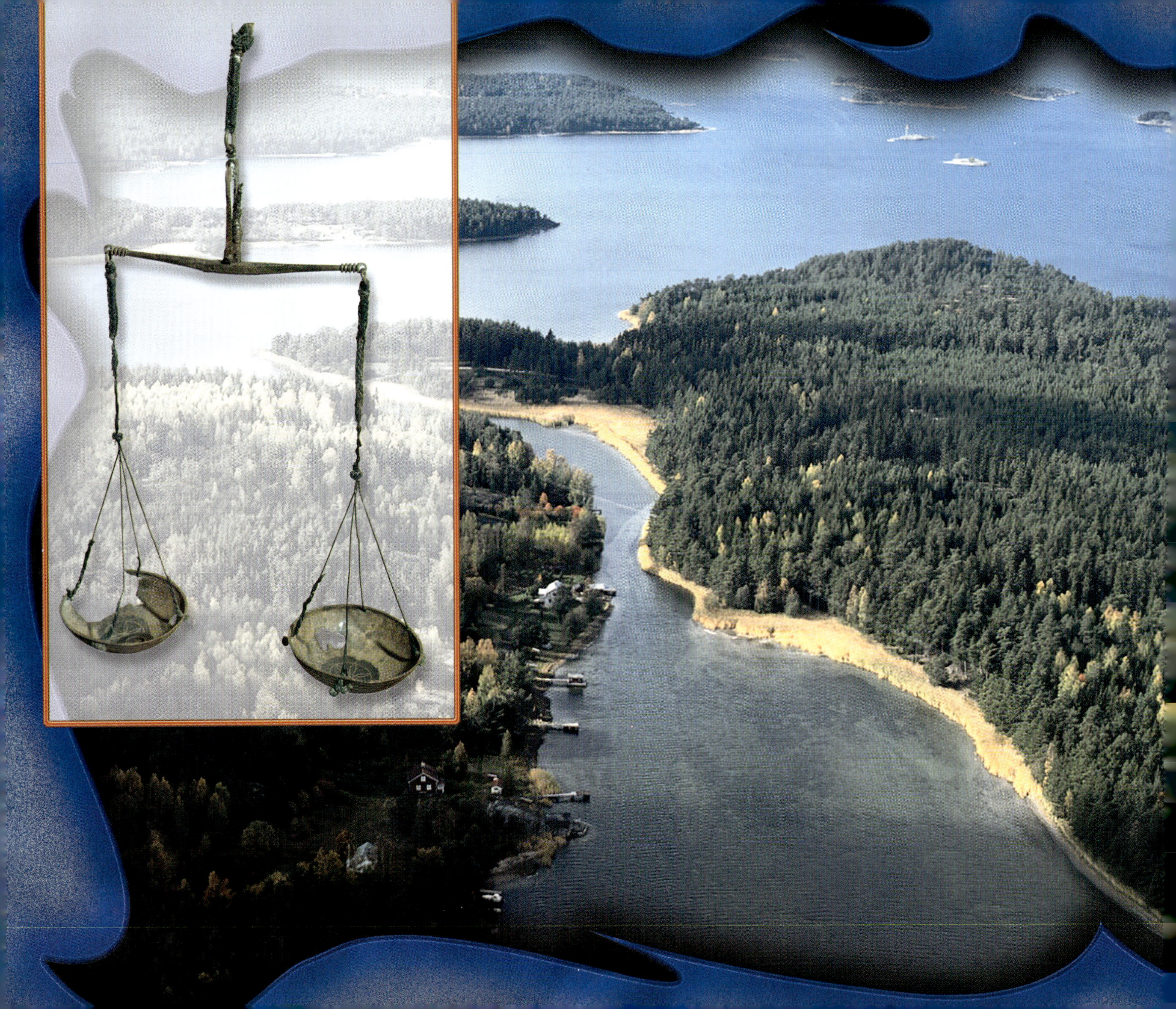

Viking Merchants

Much local and foreign trade took place among the Norse as simple exchanges of goods. This was known as bartering. Norse traders preferred to exchange goods for silver, and they bought foreign goods with silver. They weighed the silver with **scales**. Scales have been found buried in Viking graves all over northern Europe. Many Viking **merchants** traveled by horseback and visited people's homes to sell silk and other **luxury** goods, or everyday items such as salt. Norse traders came to realize trading would be easier if they built special places that were protected from raiders. Traders from many different places all could meet in safety to trade their goods. Scandinavia's towns and cities grew from trading centers.

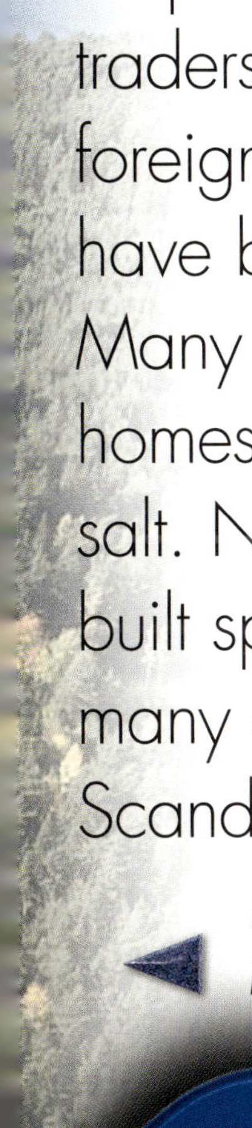

Harbors, such as this one in Finland, a Scandinavian neighbor, provided both safety and passage for Viking trade ships. Many Norse traders carried scales, like the one shown at the far left. Scales were used for weighing silver.

Viking Goods for Sale

All Norse people needed something to trade. They traded everyday things that Norse farming families could grow or make. This included preserved meat or fish, honey, ale, bread, and wool cloth. **Timber**, iron weapons, and ships were traded, also. Some people made a living by trading only one particular kind of good, such as dried fish, furs, or slaves. What they sold depended a lot on where they lived. For example, the northern parts of Sweden and Norway had many animals that could be hunted or trapped for their furs.

The museum exhibit at the left shows Norse traders and their goods. Some of the items traded by the Norse people were weapons, like the sword in the small photo, and even ships, like the Gokstad, which is on exhibit at the Viking Ship Museum in Denmark.

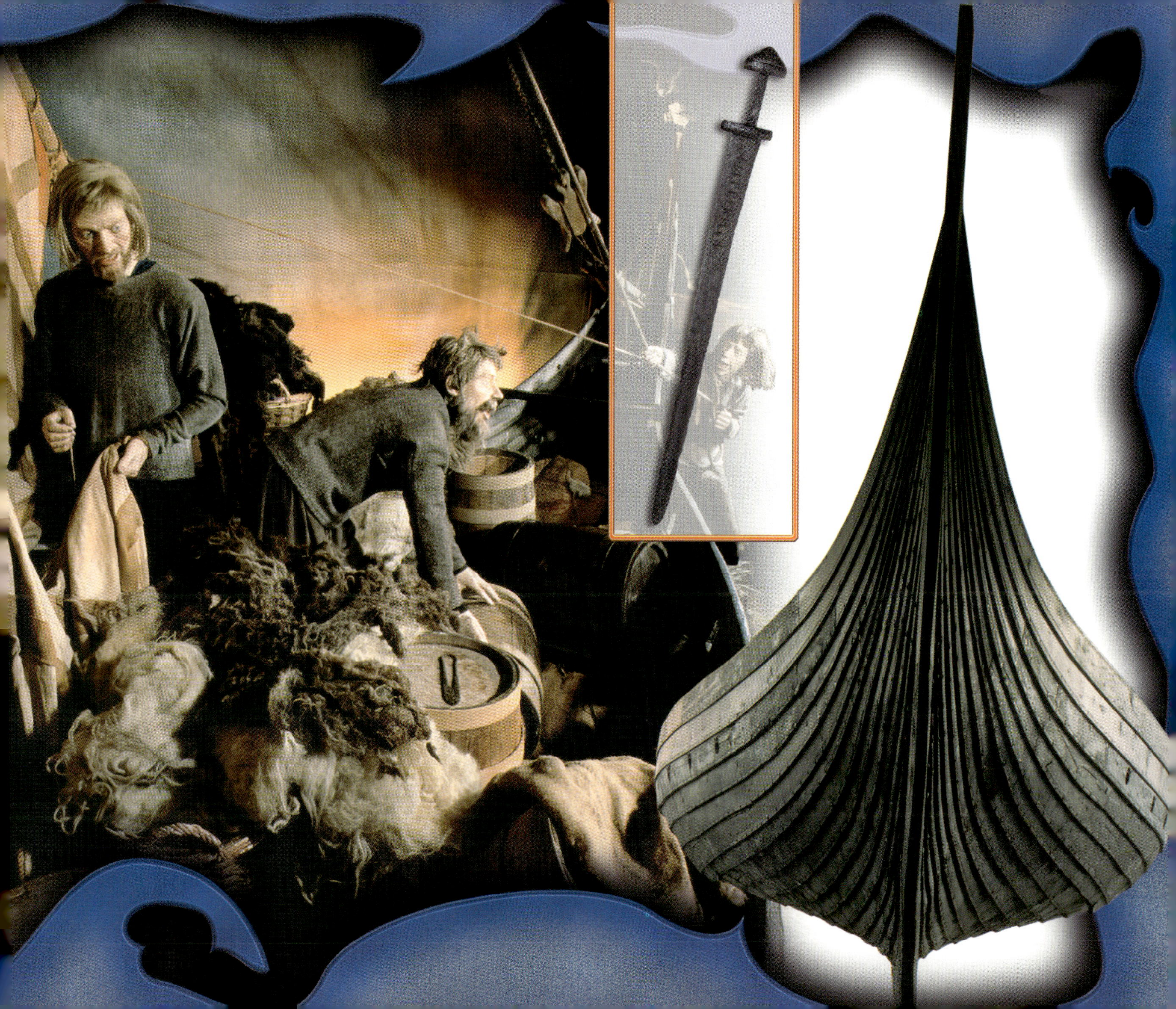

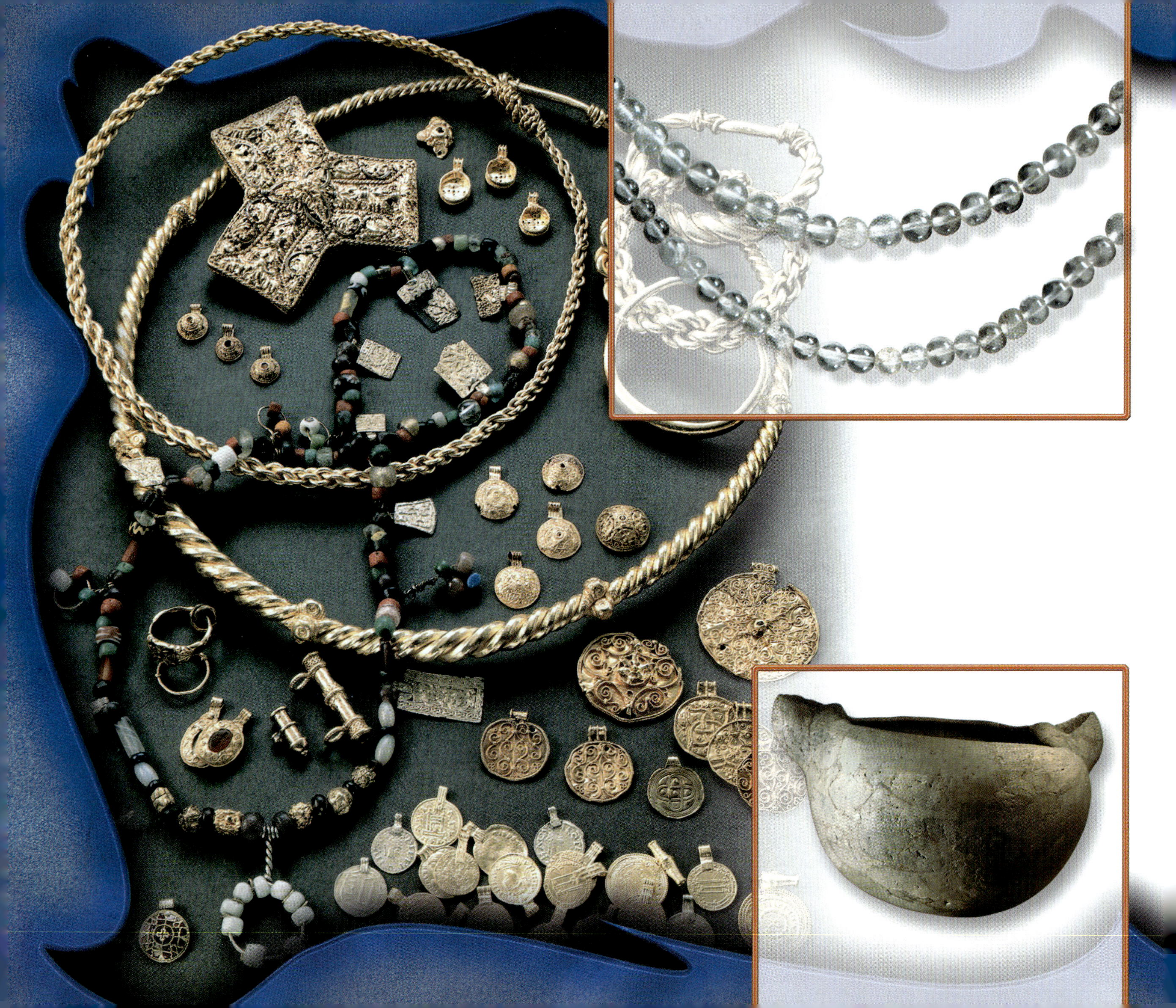

Imported Goods

Grapes couldn't grow in the cold countries of Scandinavia. If Vikings wanted wine, they imported it from warmer, southern countries. They could make pots from clay and drinking cups from wood or cow's horn. If they wanted to drink from glass, then they imported it from the Rhineland, in Germany. All kinds of luxury goods came from the East. Crystal beads and rich, silk cloth came from China. Silver came from Arabia and spices from Persia in the Middle East. The Norse exchanged slaves, weapons, furs, and honey for these luxuries.

The small photo at the top of the page shows beautiful rock crystal beads that Vikings brought back from the East. The collection of gold coins, jewelry, and colored beads were part of the Hon Hoard. This treasure was found in Norway and contained items from many different countries. The small pottery bowl, at the bottom of the page, was found in Denmark.

Scandinavian Trading Centers

The trading center at Birka, Sweden, was surrounded by wooden walls with towers at the top. Birka was a rich trading center where furs, ivory, luxury cloths, and glassware were sold. Birka was abandoned in the late tenth century.

Foreign traders traveled great distances to bring their goods to several Norse trading centers. All trading centers were under the protection of a king. Vikings attacked these centers as they did foreign cities. There were many Norse trading centers. Hedeby, which is now part of Germany, was protected by a 30-foot (9-m) **rampart** on all sides, except where it faced the water. It had a craftsman's section where pottery, jewelry, cloth, tools, and weapons were made for sale. As bigger and better trading centers were built, trading became an acceptable way for Vikings to become wealthy. When this happened, the Viking Age drew to a close.

Glossary

craftsmen (KRAFTS-min) Skilled and creative workers.
currency (KUR-un-see) Money.
essential (ih-SEN-shul) Extremely important.
fleets (FLEETS) Many ships under the command of one person.
foreign (FOR-in) Outside one's own country.
fortified (FOR-teh-fyd) Made stronger or more secure.
hoards (HORDZ) Hidden treasures or supplies.
invasions (in-VAY-zhunz) The conquering of other lands and people.
luxury (LUK-shuh-ree) Something that is nice or expensive but not really needed.
merchants (MUR-chints) People who sell or barter things.
monasteries (MAH-nuh-ster-eez) Houses where men who have taken religious vows live and work.
monks (MUNKS) Men who have taken religious vows and who live in a monastery.
rampart (RAM-part) A large wall or barrier.
resources (REE-sors-ez) Supplies or sources of energy or useful materials.
scales (SKAYLZ) Instruments used for weighing and measuring.
Scandinavia (skan-dih-NAY-vee-ah) Northern Europe, in particular Norway, Sweden, and Denmark.
slaves (SLAYVZ) People who are "owned" by other people and are forced to work for them.
timber (TIM-bur) Wood that is cut and used for building houses, ships, and other wooden objects.
tribal (TRY-buhl) Relating to groups of people who share the same customs, language, and ancestors.

Index

B
Baltic Sea, 10
bartering, 17

C
Charles the Bald, 9
China, 21
Constantinople, 13

D
danegeld, 9
Denmark, 5, 6

E
England, 6

G
Germany, 10, 21, 22

H
hacksilver, 14
Hedeby, 22

L
Lindisfarne, 6

N
Norway, 5, 6, 18

O
Oleg the Wise, 13

R
Russia, 10, 13

S
Scandinavia, 5, 14, 17, 21
Sweden, 5, 6, 18

U
Ukraine, 10

Web Sites

To learn more about Viking raiders and traders, check out these Web sites:
www.pbs.org/wgbh/nova/vikings/
www.sciam.com/1998/0298issue/0298hale.html